14234

636.08
POP
　　Pope, Joyce
　　　Taking care of your
　　rabbit

DATE DUE			
OCT 2 9 1988			
SEP 2 - 1995			
JUL 19 '95			
APR. 2 3 2005			

WITHDRAWN

TAKING CARE OF YOUR

RABBIT

Joyce Pope

Series consultant: Michael Findlay

Photographs by: Sally Anne Thompson
and R T Willbie/Animal Photography

Franklin Watts

London   New York   Toronto   Sydney

The author
Joyce Pope is Enquiries Officer of the Zoology
Department at the British Museum of Natural History
and also gives regular public lectures to children and
adults on a wide range of subjects.

She is involved with conservation groups and has
written many books on a variety of topics including
European animals, pets and town animals. She is an
enthusiastic pet owner herself and currently keeps
small mammals, two dogs, a cat and a horse.

The consultant
Michael Findlay is a qualified veterinary surgeon whose
involvement has been mainly with pet animals. He is
now an advisor to a pharmaceutical company. He is
involved with Crufts Dog Show each year and is a
member of the Kennel Club. He is president of several
Cat Clubs and is Chairman of the Feline Advisory
Bureau. He currently has three Siamese cats and two
Labrador dogs.

© 1987 Franklin Watts
First published in Great
Britain in 1987 by
Franklin Watts
12a Golden Square
London W1

First published in the
United States of America
by
Franklin Watts Inc.
387 Park Avenue South
New York
N.Y. 10016

UK edition:
ISBN 0 86313 413 0
US edition:
ISBN 0–531–10189–4
Library of Congress
Catalog Card Number:
85–52085

Designed by
Ben White
Illustrated by
Hayward Art Group

Printed in Belgium

Acknowledgments
The photographers and publishers would like to thank
Mr Jim Rowe, Lynton Pet Shop, Gloucester;
Hutchcraft, Barton Street, Gloucester; Miss Franki
Goddard, Bristol Rabbit Rescue; Gloucester and
District Rabbit Club and the families and their rabbits
who participated in the photography for this book.

Special thanks are also due to Vana Haggerty, Rabbit
Breeder, exhibitor and rabbit care advisor, for her
valuable assistance in the preparation of this book.

14234

TAKING CARE OF YOUR

RABBIT

Contents

Introducing pets

People like to keep pets. They are often good company and they can be an interesting part of our lives. By watching them and caring for them we can find out how other creatures use the world that we often think of as ours.

▽ The best sort of animal to keep as a pet is one that is not too large, but neither should it be so small that you cannot handle and stroke it safely. A pet should trust you and be able to return your affection.

Petkeepers' code

1 A pet is not a toy, but a living creature which has its own feelings and emotions.

2 A pet must be fed and given fresh water every day.

3 A pet must have its own living place which must be kept clean.

4 A pet may need to be groomed regularly.

5 A pet relies on you to care for it if it is ill.

6 You are responsible for your pet and you must see that it does not bother or harm anybody else.

◁ Rabbits are usually thought of as animals that have to be kept out of doors, but they can make very good household pets. Although they are shy, rabbits are also naturally inquisitive. You must be sure that they cannot get out of your house or garden as they might get hurt or killed.

5

What is a rabbit?

A rabbit is a plant-eating animal. It has long ears and a very short tail, which is not used to balance or to hold on with. It has large hind legs, and unlike most other creatures, it hops.

A rabbit has large eyes, placed on the sides of its head, and can see behind almost as well as it can see ahead.

▽ The biggest kind of tame or domestic rabbit is the Commercial White. This may weigh up to 22lb (10kg) and is used mainly for its meat and fur. The smallest of the tame rabbits is the Netherlands Dwarf which weighs as little as 2lb (1kg).

◁ In some tame breeds the fur is long and thick. The Angora rabbit has fur so long and fine that it is used to produce a sort of very soft wool. But they do not make good pets, because they need a lot of grooming.

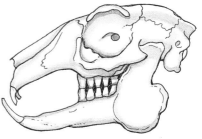

△ A rabbit nibbles its food with large teeth in the front of its mouth. At one time people thought that rabbits were very much like rodents, such as squirrels, which are also nibblers.

But rabbits' teeth are different from those of rodents – they have two tiny teeth behind the main incisors in the upper jaw. Because of this and many other differences in their bodies, scientists classify rabbits in a separate group, called the Lagomorphs.

Pet rabbits have a lot of wild relatives from many parts of the world. Some of the big ones are known as hares. Tame rabbits are all descended from the European wild rabbit which is a creature that lives in groups in burrows under the ground.

They originally came from the dry plains of Spain but once they were tamed they were taken and released in other countries. Now they are common in much of Europe and also in Australia.

Tame rabbits differ from their wild ancestors in their color, which may be white, black, gray or ginger or a mixture of shades rather than grayish brown. Some kinds of tame rabbits are much bigger than wild rabbits, while others are tiny.

Rabbits make good pets

Not all rabbits are suitable to keep as pets. The very big breeds, for instance, can be difficult to handle. Grooming the very long-haired kinds takes a great deal of time every day. But in general rabbits make good pets because they are medium-sized animals. They can be picked up and stroked without much danger of being frightened or hurt.

△ The Himalayan rabbit has white fur except for its dark colored feet, ears and nose.

▽ Tan rabbits are small to medium-size rabbits which make good pets. This coloring black and tan is most common.

Rabbits are quiet and gentle, so they are not likely to hurt you. They are clean animals and generally do not smell bad to us.

Although they must have some space to exercise, they do not need a great deal of room or have to be taken out for walks every day.

It is possible to buy a rabbit quite cheaply and, once you have it, the cost of feeding it will not be great.

If you make sure that you get a healthy pet it will probably suffer no trouble from diseases. If you look after it well it will probably live for at least five years and perhaps for twice as long as that.

▽ This is a young Flemish giant. This rabbit grows to over 12lbs (6kg) in weight. They need a lot of room and must have a large hutch.

◁ The Dwarf lop-eared weighs about $4\frac{1}{2}$lb (2kg). This rabbit is molting, which happens several times a year.

9

◁ Putting the finishing touches to a home-made hutch. The hutch should be on legs. This will protect the animal against damp and also from pests such as rats and mice. The sleeping quarters should take about one third of the length.

▽ The roof should slope slightly and should project in the front by at least 5in (12cm). Cover the roof with roofing felt. Protect the floor with a sheet of metal or hard plastic. There should be no ledges for the rabbit to gnaw, or it will quickly destroy its home.

The first things to be sure of when you decide to keep a rabbit are that you have enough space, indoors or out, and enough time to look after it properly.

The next thing is to get your parents' permission to keep a rabbit as a pet. You must also be sure that you can afford to get the right food and bedding for your pet.

If you keep your rabbit as an outdoor pet, you will need a cage or hutch for it. Most ready-made hutches are far too small, so it is best to make your own (probably with the help of an adult).

It should be at least 4ft (130cm) long, 2ft (60cm) high and 2ft (60cm) broad. If you decide to keep one of the large breeds the cage will need to be bigger still. It should be made of strong wood and covered with roofing shingles.

Do not place it in a drafty spot, nor in direct sun, as rabbits may suffer from heatstroke.

△ Whatever the type of hutch you use, you will need to get enough bedding so that your rabbits will be comfortable in their hutch. The best floor covering is wood chips, peat or shredded paper (but not newspaper). Use some straw, or hay in the sleeping area.

Keeping a rabbit indoors

△ You may allow your pet rabbit to sit on the furniture, but it should also have a sleeping box. This should be placed out of any drafts and lined with soft material and hay.

A rabbit makes a good indoor pet and can be allowed to run free much of the time, at least in a limited area. It will need a sleeping box which will be the place where it can rest at any time.

Like cats, rabbits do not foul their dens and they can be trained to use a litter tray. You should place this near to the rest box.

△ Rabbits will soon learn to use a litter tray, but you must remember to clean it out each day.

If you keep a rabbit as an indoor pet you must be sure that any fire is properly guarded. You must also take care that a rabbit kept indoors does not nibble things, especially wires, such as electric cables.

You can buy various preparations that, though they do not smell to us, taste nasty to animals. A small amount placed on danger points in the room will protect the house and also the rabbit.

You must also be very careful that the rabbit does not escape, as it will soon become confused and might even get run over.

▽ Rabbits kept indoors make very good pets and become very tame. If you have a cat or a dog you must be careful that it is not allowed in the room while the rabbit is free. Although cats or dogs may eventually learn to be friendly, they are natural hunters and might hurt the rabbit.

Choosing a rabbit

The best way to find a pet rabbit is to look in a local newspaper for details of when a rabbit show is due to be held nearby. At a show you will be able to see different breeds looking their best. You can talk to the breeders about their animals, and they may sell them.

If you can buy a rabbit at a show it is almost certain to be in good condition. It will probably be cheaper than one bought from elsewhere.

▽ If you go to a show just to look at the rabbits you will be able to see all the colors and coat types of the different breeds and decide which one you would most like to keep yourself. You can take the address of the breeder and perhaps go to see the rest of the animals. Often, rabbit breeders advertize in local newspapers.

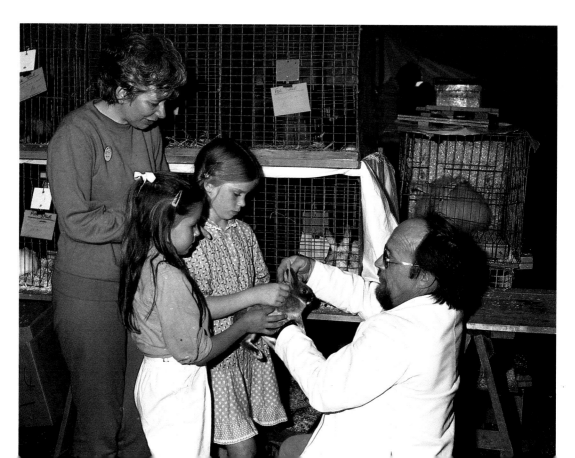

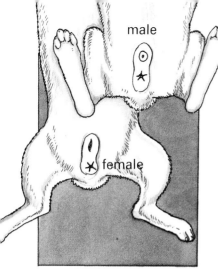

△ The breeder will tell you the sex of the animals. The female is shown on the left, the male on the right.

▷ You can choose a rabbit in a pet shop. Always use a lined carrying box to take it home in.

If you cannot go to a rabbit show, you can usually find rabbits in pet shops. These are often cross-bred and it is not always easy to know how big these baby rabbits will grow. If you get one rabbit, a buck (male), usually makes a better pet. If you decide to buy two, make sure they are both does (females).

It is best to get young rabbits, about 6–8 weeks old which will settle down well with you. Make sure that they are healthy. A rabbit with a scabby skin, dirty ears or a runny nose is almost certainly unwell.

△ A healthy rabbit looks alert and plump, with bright eyes and shining fur.

Rabbits in their new home

You will probably want to play with your new pets as soon as you get them home. But the best thing is to be patient and let them settle down for a while.

Everything is strange to them so give them a chance to get to know their new surroundings little by little. You should put them gently into the hutch or resting box that you have prepared for them with food and plenty of warm bedding.

△ Your new rabbit will probably be suspicious of you at first but if you have a carrot or some other tidbit you can coax it to come to you. Soon it will do so looking for the treat that you may have.

△ Never pick a rabbit up by its ears. Hold it by the scruff of the neck with one hand and support its rear end with the other.

△ When your rabbit is used to being picked up you can carry it about. Always support its body on your forearm.

Rabbits are quite shy animals and are easily frightened. You must be careful not to make loud noises near them, especially during their first few days in your family.

You should also keep other pets away, particularly dogs and cats. This may seem a nuisance, but it will help the rabbits to feel at ease. They will become tame much more readily if you treat them in this way.

Talk quietly to rabbits when you approach. They will quickly learn the sound of your voice and soon you will be able to stroke and handle them. When you pick them up you must always beware the sharp claws on their hind feet.

△ Once a rabbit is confident that you will not hurt or frighten it, it will allow you to stroke and cuddle it. But remember how big and strong you are compared to your pet. You must always be gentle with it.

Exercise for your rabbit

Pet rabbits need exercise. This is not only to prevent them from becoming fat, but also because they will see and smell different things as they move about and this adds interest to their lives.

If your pets have been in a hutch all winter, check the droppings after the rabbits have been out. If the droppings are loose, put the rabbits back in the hutch.

▽ Be sure that the sleeping box is waterproof and raised on bricks. There must be plenty of dry hay for bedding, in case the nights become chilly.

If you put your rabbits on new spring grass, leave them out for only thirty minutes at first. This will prevent rabbits from eating too much fresh grass which can cause diarrhea and may become a major health problem.

If you have enough space, you can make a garden run for your rabbits. The wire mesh walls do not need to be more than three feet high, but you must bury the base several inches in the ground otherwise your pets may tunnel out. The run should include a sleeping box and a length of drain pipe which will make an artificial tunnel. There should also be food and water and a piece of hard wood for the animals to gnaw on.

If you cannot leave your rabbits in an open run, you could make a morant or ark hutch. This is a triangular hutch with a wire covered run attached to it.

△ Move the outdoor run every few days and make sure there is some shade and water.

▽ A morant or ark hutch, which should be moved about so rabbits have fresh grazing.

◁ **1** Pellets, a concentrated food for rabbits. This is a complete food, so make sure you give your rabbit plenty of water.
2 Dry rabbit mix.
3 Flaked corn, which is used in mixed rabbit food but it's not wise to feed on its own.
4 Molasses mix. Besides these foods rabbits should have plenty of hay in a rack in the hutch, which can also be used for bedding.

Rabbits are plant eaters and never feed on meat of any kind.

They need a variety of different foods such as dry food, hay and fresh vegetables or grasses. In this way they can have a healthy, balanced diet.

They must also always have clean water. It is best to put this in a water bottle, as in open dishes the water may get dirty.

Dry food contains different sorts of grains such as oats and flaked corn. It can be bought from your pet store under the name of rabbit mix. It is also possible to buy dry food in pellet form, which is very concentrated, with grain and minerals in it.

The amount that you feed your pet depends on its size. For a small breed about a teacupful a day split into two meals is plenty. Your rabbit should always have fresh hay and vegetables.

▽ Here are some fruit and vegetables that people often think rabbits would like to eat. But spinach, lettuce, beetroot and pears are not recommended as they can cause very serious stomach upsets for rabbits. You can feed small quantities of the other food, but don't feed rabbits any raw potatoes.

Wild food

Rabbits will eat many kinds of wild plants, so you can add variety to your pets' diet by collecting wild grasses and dandelions, for them. When gathering wild food you should only take kinds of plants that you can identify. Many sorts are poisonous and some are very rare and should not be picked.

You should not pick plants near a big main road, as their leaves will be polluted by the traffic fumes. You should also be careful not to pick plants from areas which might have been sprayed with weedkiller or fouled by animals.

◁ You should always wash any green food, whether wild or cultivated, and shake it dry carefully before giving it to your rabbits. This will help to get rid of anything poisonous which may be left on the plants.

▷ Although rabbits are fond of clover, they should not be allowed to eat a lot of it as too much makes them very ill. But many other wild plants are good for them.

Rabbit hygiene

Rabbits are essentially clean animals. In the wild, they keep their burrows hygienic by depositing their droppings well away from their living places.

Tame rabbits cannot do this, so it is up to their owners to clean out the hutches. This helps to keep the animals healthy, as well as clean.

▽ Rabbits groom themselves regularly. As well as this, it is a good idea to brush your rabbits weekly with a baby brush. You will help to remove any shed hairs and you can see any parasites or skin diseases in their early stages.

△ When cleaning out your rabbits' hutch scrape any droppings into a container and dispose of them.

△ Because rabbits eat their bedding, you must put some fresh hay in the sleeping quarters every day.

The main part of the hutch should be cleaned out every day. Droppings and any wet floor covering should be scraped out using a small hoe or similar tool and new floor covering put down. This can be peat, wood chips or shredded paper, but do not use newspaper or sawdust.

The hay in the sleeping area should be changed every week, although a little of the old bedding should be put back so that the rabbits have a familiar smell to return to. In summer time scrub the hutch out with a disinfectant. Be sure it's dry before you return your pet to it.

△ After cleaning out the hutch rinse out your rabbits' food bowls. The water bottle should be cleaned and refilled. Always wash your hands after handling your pets or cleaning out the hutch.

Rabbit health

If you house and feed your rabbit properly, it will probably be healthy for the whole of its life.

But if your pet has lost its appetite, its coat is looking dull and untidy, it has a runny nose or its droppings show that it has diarrhea, take it to your vet as quickly as possible, as many rabbit diseases are very difficult to cure.

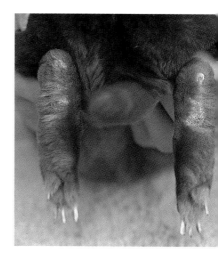

△ This rabbit has sore hocks caused by being kept in the wrong conditions. It is usually found in Rex rabbits, as they need a really thick layer of wood shavings on the hutch floor.

◁ The gnawing or incisor teeth in the front of a rabbit's mouth grow throughout the animal's life. Usually these teeth are worn down to the right length through eating. If the teeth grow far too long, take the rabbit to the vet as the animal may not be able to eat properly.

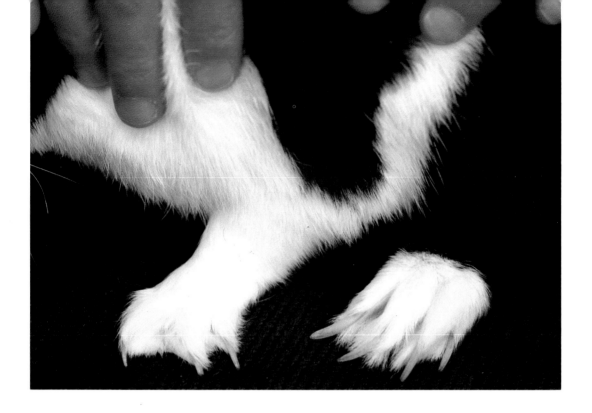

One of the worst diseases of rabbits is myxomatosis. This can be passed to pet rabbits by wild rabbit fleas. If wild rabbits get into the garden where your pets play, you should ask your vet to protect your pets with a vaccination.

Mucoid enteritis shows itself in diarrhea containing mucus. It is often found in rabbits which do not have enough hay to eat, so it can usually be prevented by a proper diet. A serious disease of rabbits is called snuffles. Rabbits of any age can get a cold, which may turn to pneumonia. If a rabbit seems sick, separate it from the others and keep it warm until the vet can see it.

△ Rabbits' claws grow like our finger nails and if they are not attended to may curve right round as has happened here.

△ Your vet will show you how to trim your rabbit's claws so that they can be kept in good condition.

Understanding your rabbit

By understanding your rabbit's world you will become a better animal keeper.

You will also get more enjoyment as you begin to learn how your pet reacts to things and what it means by different postures and expressions. This will help you to recognize when it is frightened or ill and when to help.

△ If you introduce a new rabbit to a rabbit you already have, don't leave them alone together, as the older one may attack the younger one. Keep them in separate hutches where they can see each other and then they may become used to each other.

You can find out about your rabbit by watching and timing the things that it does. Discover when it grooms itself. Does it do so in the morning or after it has been fed? How long does it take?

Find out about its sleep patterns. Does it catnap, or does it sleep soundly for long periods? What are its favorite foods? Does it hoard them? How fast does it grow? Record all of these things in a rabbit diary. It could make the basis of a good science project.

▽ You can discover your rabbit's favorite food by seeing which it eats first if you offer it two different tidbits at the same time. You may find that it prefers different foods at different times of day or year.

▷ You can discover how quickly your rabbit grows if you weigh it regularly. Measure the length of its hind foot when you first get it. Find out how much this grows as the rabbit increases in size and weight.

Checklist

 Check before you buy a rabbit:

1 That you have your parents' permission.
2 That you have space to keep a rabbit.
3 That you have time and can afford to keep it.

 Check daily:

1 That your rabbit is given two adequate meals including dry food, fresh fruit and vegetables, and hay, some of which is its bedding.
2 That your rabbit has clean drinking water.
3 That the cage is cleaned of recent droppings.
4 That the rabbit's food bowls are rinsed clean.
5 That your rabbit is in general good health (you should see this when you stroke it or play with it).
6 That your rabbit exercises outside its hutch.

 Check weekly:

1 That the loose floor covering in the cage and bedding in the sleeping area is new and clean.
2 That your pet's water bottle is washed out.
3 That you have enough food in store for the next week.

 Check monthly:

1 That your rabbit's hutch is properly scrubbed out with disinfectant, rinsed thoroughly and is dry before the animal is returned to it.
2 That your pet's claws and teeth are not growing too long.

Questions and answers

Q What is the rabbit's scientific name?
A *Oryctolagus cuniculus.*

Q How many sorts of tame rabbits are there?
A There are about 35 different breeds of tame rabbits. These are all members of the same species, so they can all interbreed. The result of this would be cross-breeds or mongrels, but they still make very good pets.

Q What is the biggest kind of tame rabbit?
A The British Giant may weigh up to 22lb (10kg).

Q Which is the smallest kind of tame rabbit?
A There are several small breeds, but the Netherlands Dwarf, which weighs only about 2lb (1kg) is the smallest.

Q How long does a rabbit live?
A If you feed and look after your rabbit properly, it would probably live for 5 or 6 years. Some may survive for longer than this. Some pet rabbits have lived for 11 years.

Q Are there any diseases that I might catch from my pet rabbit?
A There is no common rabbit disease that is normally caught by human beings or other pets such as cats and dogs.

Index